T0129569

TRUTHS TO LIVE BY

THOUGHTS AND INSIGHTS

CAROLYN HIGHTOWER

BALBOA.
PRESS

A DIVISION OF HAY HOUSE

Balboa Press books may be ordered through booksellers or by contacting:

Balboa Press
A Division of Hay House
1663 Liberty Drive
Bloomington, IN 47403
www.balboapress.com
1 (877) 407-4847

Because of the dynamic nature of the Internet, any web addresses or
links contained in this book may have changed since publication and
may no longer be valid. The views expressed in this work are solely those
of the author and do not necessarily reflect the views of the publisher,
and the publisher hereby disclaims any responsibility for them.

The author of this book does not dispense medical advice or prescribe
the use of any technique as a form of treatment for physical, emotional,
or medical problems without the advice of a physician, either directly
or indirectly. The intent of the author is only to offer information
of a general nature to help you in your quest for emotional and
spiritual well-being. In the event you use any of the information in
this book for yourself, which is your constitutional right, the author
and the publisher assume no responsibility for your actions.

Any people depicted in stock imagery provided by Getty Images are
models, and such images are being used for illustrative purposes only.
Certain stock imagery © Getty Images.

Print information available on the last page.

ISBN: 978-1-9822-2519-3 (sc)
ISBN: 978-1-9822-2520-9 (e)

Balboa Press rev. date: 01/03/2020

ABOUT THE AUTHOR

She started her journey about twelve years ago, when she woke up one morning and just simply asked, who really she was and why was she here. Unknowingly to what she had opened up to let come though was unimaginable. Many unbelievable experiences have occurred that have taken her into where the soul resides. The dark canvas of the mind where there are no thoughts, no identity, just peace. The mind alone cannot know this. When she was in her thirties she would lay down in the afternoon, fall asleep and leave her

body. At that time she didn't understand that she was not the body or the mind. After many years of believing she was just this body and mind, she could not believe this any longer. A profound understanding had come over her and took her into the depths of the one being we all truly are. She died on the sand of Kauai beach in 2017. She was aware that the pain was gone instantly, but was not aware of any thoughts or memories or that she had left the physical world, just a peaceful awareness was present. She came back to the physical world virtually unharmed. People tell her it was the lifeguards who saved her. The true understanding is that we are all one and that the one self is in all of us. The one self is the one that orchestrated the whole event. There is no other.

If you want to feel contentment, feel your pain.

When you realize you lack nothing, the whole world belongs to you.

There is no greater experience of love than the love that is felt when you let go of control and trust that life will take care of you. You will have to become totally vulnerable to life and not have fear as your constant companion.

It's not easy to quiet a programmed mind that's been dubbed for centuries.

To get out of this stale paradigm, we have to think for ourselves and not be influenced by centuries of fearful thinking.

When we graduate from smallness to the recognition of our greatness so that our internal joy comes from the pleasure of giving and loving, then we are really invulnerable to loss. When the source of happiness is found within, we are all immune to the losses of the world.

The mind is not a thing; it is an interaction. Like the brain, the mind is the whole interaction event of human beings in relationship with the world.

Consciousness shifts as the sense of self does.

When you let go of fear, your life gets exciting.

What doesn't exist can't be done over, don't dwell on the past.

TRUTHS TO LIVE BY

Attachment is not love.

The mind is nothing, so how can it know anything?

When you disassociate the mind from the false self, you no longer listen to the mind.

Depression is living in the past. Orneriness and anxiety are living in the future. The present is peace.

The screen behind the movie is what's real, not the movie.

The ego is only a thought.

Your life is not about you.

When you stop looking, you find.

When you stop worrying, things turn out okay or fall into place.

All life forms are only visiting here.

Take a look at what you are not. This wakes you up to what you really are.

The reasonable person adapts oneself to the world; the unreasonable individual persists in trying to adapt the world to him or her.

Make a life, not a living. Money is love.

We come into our true beings gradually, through a process of evolution.

You are the universe, awakening to your own existence.

The mind believes that awareness shares the limits and, therefore, the destiny of the body. This apparent mixture of awareness with the properties and limitations of

TRUTHS TO LIVE BY

the body results in the separate self and ego that most people believe and feel themselves to be.

When you awake to reality, you no longer have somewhere more important to be.

If your life is not a living realization of your awareness, then fear is your reality.

Your true being has your best interests at heart.

When you stop struggling with the way things are, your consciousness soars into uncontainable freedom.

All human-made beliefs are flawed because they were created by flawed humans.

All that remains when you die is your awareness.

TRUTHS TO LIVE BY

You are not the mind and body; you only think you are.

Guilt and fear are the only enemies of humans.

Troublemakers improve thinking.

We are undeveloped souls walking around in the dark.

Your life is not about you; it's about how you show up in this world.

It's not easy being divine until it is.

You are the same energy as that little ant. Humans have been given the responsibility of evolving.

Trust that the tool kit will be there.

TRUTHS TO LIVE BY

The intelligence that you have does not come from the small self you think you are.

When you're attached to this world, you hang on. When you're not, you move on.

Expect everything that is wonderful, and accept everything that is not.

Believe in extraordinary things.

You are in your own way.

Go beyond what you can imagine.

You are much more than you think you are.

Imagine the impossible because everything is possible.

Thought does not need our attention.

The present moment is all there is.

TRUTHS TO LIVE BY

It takes an enormous amount of audacity to let go of the future.

Silence is a place where you don't need anything from this world or this life. Rest there.

Freedom does not mean feeling good all the time.

Freedom is to give everything; hold nothing back.

This is the moment right here, right now.

Give up the future.

Be content even on the worst day of your life.

You can only be afraid if you think you know. Innocence is not knowing.

TRUTHS TO LIVE BY

Your life is an amazing journey into the unknown.

We are always trying to get something from something that doesn't exist.

You can't run away from the agitation of the mind; you face it.

Nothing is ever right or wrong, happy or sad. It just is. You change it by how you perceive it.

The soul comes here to love through you, as you.

Why does God have to wake up if God is already awake? God doesn't, but the identity of yourself that you have accepted does.

TRUTHS TO LIVE BY

When the true self is fully awake, there is no suffering left. Then you recognize that there never was any suffering.

Freedom is here right now. Freedom is who you are; you allow it.

The one self comes here to the physical to experience being you.

The ego thinks it's getting something for itself. The soul knows it already has it.

Something that is unreal, like the future, is unpredictable.

The universe loves and cherishes your very existence.

The cosmic joke is that there are no chains binding us.

TRUTHS TO LIVE BY

We are bound by an invisible fence that exist only in our minds.

Be as happy with pain as with joy because they're the same.

The false identity doesn't wake up; it falls away. It surrenders.

When fear arises, seemingly from nowhere, the mind is experiencing, not the soul. That is being soulless.

All flesh goes back to where it came from. The soul never left.

Evolution is not moving up. It's waking up.

Don't expect anything, and accept everything.

Get out of the way. Let your soul live through you as you.

Surrender is the only way to be fully awake at all times.

Abundance does not come from the physical.

Abundance is not something you get; it's something you feel.

Waking up is about never leaving this very moment. This moment is the only thing that is real, and it's always here, always present. There are no past or present moments.

The stuff one's consciousness is made of is the stuff of the world. We are the world that we perceive.

Your sense of separation and individuality is an illusion.

TRUTHS TO LIVE BY

The ego is nothing more than a thought.

The world is in you; you are not in the world.

You think you are born and die, but the world appears and disappears.

The death of the personal self is the only possibility for seeing liberation. The self has to disappear.

Awareness is everywhere. It's all there is.

Awakening and liberation are about waking to the dream that is ordinary life.

What's missing is the primal sense of unity that was present when you were born.

Oneness is playing at being a character.

TRUTHS TO LIVE BY

You're so much less than a person. But you're so much more than that as well because you are awareness itself.

Recognizing a problem as a doorway requires you to let the world fall away in the midst of your resistance to whatever is happening.

Everything you think you know is secondhand knowledge. Everything you know without thinking is what you actually know.

You can only recognize illusion when you stop wanting to be one.

Detachment does not mean that you should own nothing but that nothing should own you.

TRUTHS TO LIVE BY

Have the courage to see the truth and the wisdom not to react.

Trust life, and give up control. It's called faith.

There is nothing you have to do or strive for. You are already all you can be.

Meditation helps you recognize the true self in this so-convincing illustration you are in.

When people have near-death experiences, a few have said it's hell, and some say it's heaven. It's all just the fact that you're having an experience. The truth is that your true self is pure awareness, and that's all there is.

TRUTHS TO LIVE BY

Nonduality is consciousness manifesting the picture that consciousness paints. It's one picture that is constantly changing.

If you're already awake and free, you don't need to know you are.

The unknown is already known. In the not knowing, you find the known.

The mind cannot think about awareness.

Keep your attention off yourself.

You wake up in the middle of a life that was designed by your unawakened self.

The I that you are has to see itself. Give this your attention. Self-abidance. I am only I.

Can you ever be disturbed by anything that is experienced?

TRUTHS TO LIVE BY

Your happiness is prior to experience.

All we have to do is remove the limits that we have on our true being.

God is the very self of each of us.

You are not where you travel to but where you travel from.

Silent alert, not afraid, does not have an identity. You are the gap.

Stop leaving the silence that you are.

In nobodyness, there's no identity.

The intelligence that is having our experience of awaking is not separate from the intelligence of this whole glorious universe.

Suffering is a resistance to your experience.

TRUTHS TO LIVE BY

Accept your suffering, and then it will end.

All life cooperates when you give up the struggle.

Where your thoughts are, your future will also be.

There are only two places from which to come as we move through our lives. We are either coming from love, or we are coming from fear in everything that we think and do.

There's a part of you that the mind can never know.

Look through the illusion to see reality.

You can play the part of the world while staying awake, returning.

TRUTHS TO LIVE BY

Deep sleep is awareness; dreaming is the mind, awake is the body.

If you want to get rid of fear, you have to live with it.

Suffering in the mind is what pain is in the body. See that there is no separate self there.

We spend our whole lives worrying and caring for a self that isn't there.

I need nothing, but I am everything.

You, as awareness, have never come in contact with anything but yourself.

Become aware of awareness.

We are all aware of much more than we think we are.

TRUTHS TO LIVE BY

Can we become aware of awareness and rest there?

Thought shapes energy in every dimensional reality.

We don't have to learn; we just have to remember.

We see things as solid, lasting, and independent. If you do, you're dreaming.

For the ego to unravel, it has to be loved.

We suffer because we believe that things are real.

Life isn't hard; you are.

We don't see things the way they are. We see them the way we are.

TRUTHS TO LIVE BY

Blessed are the flexible for they never get bent out of shape.

Be engaged and present in the moment.

Those who look outside dream. Those who look inside awaken.

Change your attitude, change your life.

Emotion is a product of the mind. Emotions are based on your thoughts. Feelings are based on your truth. Feelings come from the soul.

Trust that life is fair and that life is good.

When you put down others, you put down yourself.

When you stop having, insisting, or trying to know, your true self starts creating.

TRUTHS TO LIVE BY

It takes a supreme amount of discipline to make no effort.

When the ego no longer has any power, nothing changes, but everything has changed.

Only good thoughts are true; they come from awareness.

Awareness is moving through you as you to wake up to a grander and grander version of self.

The advisory is the left hemisphere of the brain. The master is the right hemisphere. When you have surrendered to the master your life unfolds into a creative miracle.

The universe is designed to give you what you know.

TRUTHS TO LIVE BY

We live in a world of pure awareness. We assume there is someone experiencing. Let go of the idea that you are the one having the experience.

You cannot know who you are from the mind. The mind has to be surrendered, then you wake up to the miracle of you.

Awareness does not need an entity to be aware, without the entity, there is no experience.

Awareness has no restrictions, references, or restraints.

There are no failures, only experience. Stop letting fear make your decisions, and start letting love make them.

Printed in the United States
by Bookmasters

Printed in the United States
By Bookmasters